History of Toho Beads

From ancient times to the present day, humans have loved collecting and adorning themselves with beads.

The first beads were found objects with naturally occurring holes. Then people began to drill holes in objects like nuts, stones and shells. Eventually, glass bead making was developed. Over the years techniques improved and beautiful, more uniform beads were manufactured.

During the 1930's, the Showa era in Japan, small family businesses specializing in glass bead making began to flourish.

The Toho Bead Company was founded in 1951 and has strived to make the best beads... continually improving both their equipment and their facilities. Toho glass beads, the finest made, are used by bead artists and jewelers around the world. Their uniform size and shape and large holes make Toho beads a pleasure to use.

Toho wishes to thank their many loyal clients for their cooperation and continued support.

Features of Toho Beads

Large Holes - *The size of the holes in Toho beads allows for threading multiple strands of thread or thicker thread, increasing the variety of beadwork you can achieve.*

Light Weight - *The larger hole means less weight so you get more beads when you buy by weight. There are approximately 111,800 size 11 Toho beads per kilo.*

Toho Triangle Beads

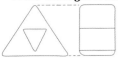

Toho Small & Large Round Beads

Cylinder Bead Color Conversion Chart

Delica	Toho Treasure	Delica	Toho Treasure	Delica	Toho Treasure	Delica	Toho Treasure
141	A-1	420	A-553	325	A-705	76	A-781
201	A-121	417	A-554	324	A-706	58	A-782
234	A-145	410	A-557	327	A-710	86	A-783
51	A-161	35	A-558	21	A-711	74	A-785
100	A-162	412	A-559	31	A-712	80	A-786
179	A-176	413	A-560	38	A-713	1	A-81
41	A-21	414	A-561	32	A-714	2	A-82
42	A-22	421	A-562	34	A-715	7	A-83
22	A-221	422	A-563	351	A-761	3	A-84
22L	A-221A	423	A-564	352	A-762	4	A-85
44	A-23	451	A-601	353	A-763	5	A-86
62	A-241	452	A-602	354	A-764	6	A-88
87	A-245	455	A-605	355	A-765	233	A-903
43	A-25	310	A-610	56	A-771	235	A-906
200	A-41	306	A-611	85	A-7 73	244	A-909
104	A-425	301	A-612	59	A-774	246	A-910
124	A-457	307	A-613	60	A-775	243	A-917
135	A-461	311	A-617	63	A-776	238	A-920
10	A-49	33	A-701	66	A-777		
411	A-551	322	A-702	70	A-779		
418	A-552	312	A-703	72	A-780		

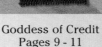

Goddess Pin

Finished size is 1¼" x 2¾"

General Materials

Beading thread and needle • Pin back
Black & Blue Pin
Worldly Goods Button #B432WB • 2 Worldly Goods Charms #C201WB
Toho Beads:
3 grams 11/0 hex beads #H28 • 3 grams 11/0 hex beads #H610
Green & Brown Pin
Worldly Goods Button #B433YB • 2 Worldly Goods Charms #C804YB
Toho Beads:
3 grams 11/0 hex beads #H84 • 3 grams 11/0 hex beads #H702
White & Gold Pin
Worldly Goods Button #B433YB • 2 Worldly Goods Charms #C702YB
Toho Beads:
3 grams 11/0 hex beads #H122 • 3 grams 11/0 hex beads #H22B

Brick Stitch

Brick stitch has a natural decrease. Every row will automatically have 1 less bead or set of beads than the previous row.
Therefore, a flat piece of brick stitch is triangular in shape.
We start with a simple stopper bead!
Row 1: Thread your needle with 48" of thread. Make an overhand knot around a bead about 12" from the end as shown in Illustration 1. Be sure to leave a 12" tail. We'll be needing it very soon…

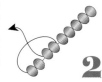

Next we'll make a 2-bead ladder. If you haven't used this method before it may help to lay your work out on a table until you get used to it. Thread on 14 light beads and 14 dark beads. Move them down to within a few inches of the stopper bead. Take your needle back through the 3rd and 4th bead from the end as shown in Illustration 2.

Pull your thread slowly. (The beads on the end will turn over.) Arrange the beads as shown in Illustration 3.

Pass your needle back through the next two beads as shown in Illustration 4. Pull your thread slowly. (The set of four beads will turn over.)
Arrange the beads as shown in Illustration number 5.
Pass your needle back through the next two beads as shown in Illustration 6. Pull your thread slowly. (The set of six beads will turn over.) Arrange the beads as shown here in Illustration 7.
Continue in this manner until all 28 beads have been added to the ladder (14 groups of two beads).
You will have to move the stopper bead farther down the tail from time to time as this method uses thread from both ends.
Row 2: Position the ladder as shown in Illustration 8.

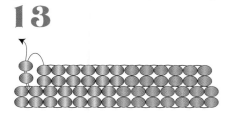

String four light beads. Notice the loops connecting each group of beads across the top edge of Row 1. Skip the loop just next to the thread and hook the needle under the second loop. Bring the needle back up through the last two beads *(Illustration 9)*.

Pass the needle back down through the first set of beads, try to catch the first loop of thread, and then bring the needle back up through the second set *(Illustrations 10 & 11)*. This 'locks' the first group of beads to the second and keeps it in line with the rest of the row.

String two beads, hook needle under next loop and bring needle back up through beads *(Illustration 12)*.

Work 3 more sets of light beads. Continue to the end of the row with dark beads. You should have 13 groups of beads in this second row - six light sets and seven dark sets *(Illustration 13)*.

Rows 3 through 13:
Row 3: work 6 dark sets and 6 light sets.
Row 4: 5 light sets and 6 dark sets.
Row 5: 5 dark sets and 5 light sets.
Row 6: 4 light sets and 5 dark sets.
Row 7: 4 dark sets and 4 light sets.
Row 8: 3 light sets and 4 dark sets.
Row 9: 3 dark sets and 3 light sets.
Row 10: 2 light sets and 3 dark sets.
Row 11: 2 dark sets and 2 light sets.
Row 12: 1 light set and 2 dark sets.
Row 13: 1 dark set and one light set.
Weave the needle back through several sets of beads to secure. Clip the thread. Remove the stopper bead from the other end. Weave the tail through several sets of beads to secure. Clip the thread. Your finished piece should look like Illustration 14.

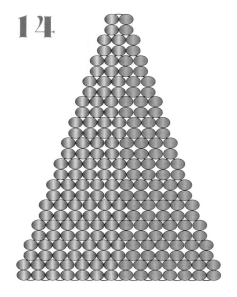

Repeat Rows 1 to 13 for the second half of the project. Do not clip thread. Instead, weave the end of the thread along one side of the triangle back to the first row. Flip the piece over and weave through the first row to the fifth group from one end *(Illustration 15)*.

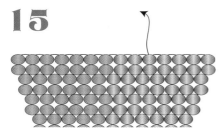

Rows 14 to 15: *(second half of pin only)* Work two more rows on this side of Row 1 as shown in Illustration 16.

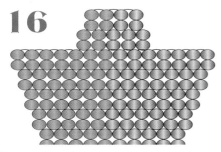

If button has a horizontal shank, attach button for head as shown in Illustration 17. Go back over your stitching several times to secure button firmly to beaded body.

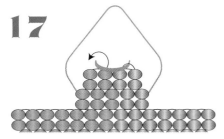

If button has a vertical shank, attach button for head as shown in Illustrations 18 & 19. Go back over your stitching several times to secure button firmly to beaded body.

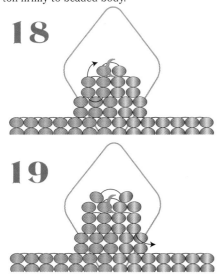

Let's face facts:
You're going to run out of thread at some point, but there's no need to panic - or to tie a knot! To end a thread, weave down through several bead groups on the rows below. Clip thread end. Cut another 36" length of thread and weave up through several bead groups on the rows below to come up out of the last group of beads you added. Weave down to end a thread, weave up to start a new one.

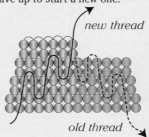

new thread

old thread

20 **Stitch the two halves together:** Line up the two halves of the body with button head facing out and stitch them together as shown in Illustration 20.

Bring needle out of top left set of beads. Add 17 beads for arm as shown in Illustration 21.

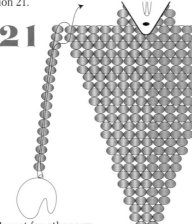

Repeat for other arm.

Position hands as shown in Illustration 22 and stitch in place on body.
Stitch pin back to back of body.

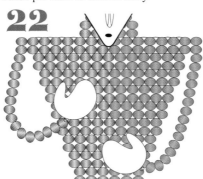

Samples made by Kim Papke and Amy Salazar

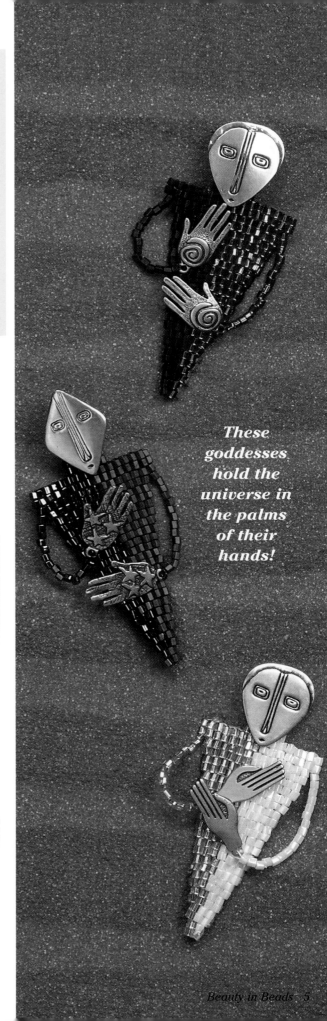

These goddesses hold the universe in the palms of their hands!

Finished size: 6" x 9"

General Materials:

9" x 15" piece of glazed kidskin • 30 sheets of 8½" x 11" paper • 12" of 1mm round leather lace • 24" of waxed linen thread • Two ⅛" diameter plastic tubes 3" long • Bone folder • Hammer and small 1½" finishing nails or drill and 1/16" bit • Beading thread and needle • Clamps

Black Journal
Worldly Goods 1¼" square wood button • Worldly Goods button #B432YB
Toho Beads:
15 grams 11/0 #610 (M) • 1 gram 11/0 #221 (A1) • 1 gram 11/0 #222 (A2) • 6 size 6/0 #610 • 6 size 6/0 #221 • 6 size 6/0 #222 • 6 Brass 6mm disk

Burgundy Journal
Worldly Goods 1¼" square wood button • Worldly Goods button #B634YB
Toho Beads:
15 grams 11/0 #222 (M) • 1 gram 11/0 #558 (A1) • 1 gram 11/0 #610 (A2) • 6 size 6/0 #610 • 6 size 6/0 #221 • 6 size 6/0 #222 • 6 Brass 6mm disk beads

Begin Rows:

Rows 1 to 2: Pour a few of the main color beads into a small shallow bowl or beading tray. Cut a 48" length of thread, thread the needle with one end. Make an overhand knot around a bead about 6" from the end as shown in Illustration 1. Be sure to leave a 6" tail. String 18 main color (M), 2 accent color 1 (A1), 16M, 2 accent color 2 (A2) and 14M beads on the thread.
Row 3: Pick up two more M beads and pass the needle back through the second pair of beads from the end *(Illustration 2)*.
This project is worked in 2 drop peyote stitch - we'll always be working with pairs of beads.

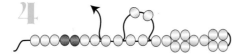

Add two more M beads as shown in Illustration 3.

Add two more M beads *(Illustration 4)*. Notice how the beads from the first row 'share' the space with the new beads?

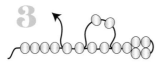

Refer to the beading pattern and word chart to complete the row.
Row 4: Reverse direction and add the first pair of this row as shown in Illustration 5.

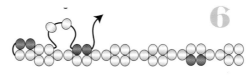

Refer to the beading pattern and word chart to complete the row.
Row 4 (l to r): 6M 1A2 6M **means**
Row 4 is worked from left to right. You stitch 6 main, 1 accent 1 and 6 main pairs of beads to complete the row.

Rows 5 - 16: Refer to the beading pattern and word chart to complete the row.

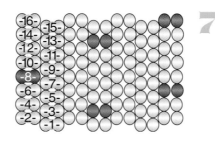

Here's a tip to help you determine which row you are on: count the rows along the edge as shown in Illustration 7.

You're going to run out of thread at some point, but there's no need to panic - or to tie a knot! - To end a thread, weave down through a few beads on the rows below and clip the end. Weave the new thread up through a few beads to come up out of the last bead you added. Weave down to end a thread, weave up to start a new one *(Illustration 8)*.

new thread

old thread

Remove the stopper bead. Fold the piece in half lengthwise, you see the edges fit together like the teeth of a zipper. Stitch the teeth together as shown in Illustration 9. The illustration shows you the thread path only - you'll tighten your thread and form the piece into a tube of course! Your finished tube should look like Illustration 10 below.

Tie the end of the thread and the tail together securely.
Slip the plastic tube into the bead tube. Add the disk and seed bead end-caps as shown in Illustration 11. Tie the loose ends of thread in a knot to secure.

Continued on page 8.

Make a journal. You can do it!

Word Chart

Rows 1 and 2: **beads** 18M 2A1 16M 2A2 14M
Row 3 (r to l): **pairs** 11M 1A1 1M
Row 4 (l to r): 6M 1A2 6M
Row 5 (r to l): 2M 1A1 10M
Row 6 (l to r): 3M 1A2 9M
Row 7 (r to l): 13M
Row 8 (l to r): 1A2 12M
Row 9 (r to l): 5M 1A1 7M

Row 10 (l to r): 12M 1 A2
Row 11 (r to l): 8M 1A1 4M
Row 12 (l to r): 9M 1A2 3M
Row 13 (r to l): 11M 1A1 1M
Row 14 (l to r): 6M 1A2 6M
Row 15 (r to l): 2M 1A1 10M
Row 16 (l to r): 3M 1A2 9M

Beading Pattern

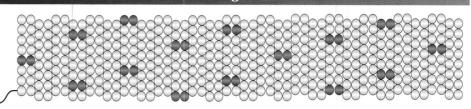

Sample made by Diane Schultz

Make journals that are sure to inspire you to record your private thoughts, creative ideas and heartfelt dreams!

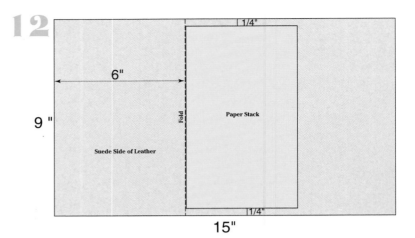

12

6"

9"

1/4"

Fold

Paper Stack

Suede Side of Leather

1/4"

15"

Continued from page 6.

Let's Make the Book

Fold 30 sheets of plain white paper in half with short sides together. Each folded sheet should measure 5½" x 8½". Crease each fold with your fingernail or a bone folder to reduce bulk.

Stack the sheets with the folded edges together.

Cut a piece of glazed kidskin 15" wide x 9" high.

Place the stack of paper on the suede side of kidskin referring to Illustration 12.

Fold the left side of the kidskin over the stack. Line up the left side of kidskin with the right side of the paper stack.

Clamp the assembly to a scrap piece of plywood. Place a scrap piece of leather between the clamps and the journal to prevent scratching or marring the surface of the kidskin. Realign the edges if necessary.

Mark the hole placement on front of journal as shown in Illustration 13.

13

1"
1/2"
3"
1/2"
1/2"
3"
1/2"
1"

Drill the the 4 holes through the leather and paper assembly with a ¹⁄₁₆" bit. Or hammer a small finishing nail through the leather and paper at each of the four points. Check alignment after completing each hole.

Remove the assembly from the clamps.

Stitch the pieces together.

Cut an 18" piece of waxed linen and thread it through a darning needle. Open the cover and fold the pages to the left. Thread one end through the second hole from top through all the pages and the front cover as shown in Illustration 14.

14

Pass the thread around one end of a beaded tube and back through the same hole going all the way through the journal and out the back cover. Bring the thread up to the top hole and pass it from the back to the front. Wrap thread around the other end of the tube and stitch back down through all layers (Illustration 15).

15

Bring the thread back up through the back cover at the second hole as shown in Illustration 16. Tighten the the threads securely around the beaded tubes and tie a knot in the ends of thread. Clip close to knot.

Repeat procedure for the second beaded tube.

16

Close the book and fold the right flap over the left. Mark hole placement for button and leather tie as shown in Illustration 17. You may wish to trim a bit off the right side if things seem a bit crowded. Punch holes with an ice pick or hammer and finishing nail.

17

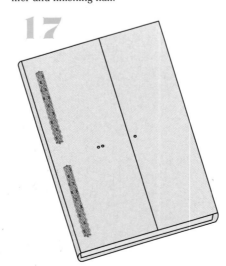

18

Place the shank of the button through the hole in the wood button as shown in Illustration 18. Stitch the button assembly to the left front cover.

Cut a 16" piece of 1mm leather lace and attach it to the hole on the right cover with a lark's head knot as shown in Illustration 19.

19

Thread on 6/0 beads and brass disk as shown in Illustration 20. Tie an overhand knot in the end of lace before trimming ends.

20

Wrap the lace around the button assembly to secure the cover.

Finished size: approximately 2½" x 4"

General Materials:

Turquoise goddess pendant • 15mm to 20mm Turquoise disk • Two 6mm Turquoise disks • Four 4mm Brass round beads • Five 6mm Brass disk beads • Beading thread and needle • .010 flexible beading wire

Sea Foam Goddess Toho Beads:
53 grams 11/0 #952
Transparent Brown Goddess Toho Beads:
53 grams 11/0 #423
Matte Metallic Brown Goddess Toho Beads:
53 grams 11/0 #702

The BIG Picture

We'll be making the bag and the flap in one long piece. When the piece is completed, you'll fold the front up and stitch the sides together. The vast majority of the bag will be worked three beads at a time with one exception - the 'hinge' or point where the flap folds down over the bag will be worked with single beads. Try to keep a light tension as you work.

Row 2: Add the first set of three beads as shown in Illustration 1.

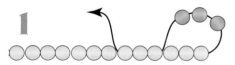

Add a second group of three beads as shown in Illustration 2. Notice how the beads from the first row 'share' the space with the new beads? Try to adjust your tension so that the row looks like Illustration 3.
Add a total of 21 groups along the first row.

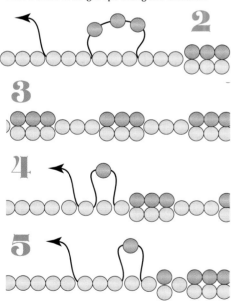

Now go back to stitching groups of three to the end of the row (Illustration 6).

Row 3:
Reverse your direction and add the first group of row 3 as shown in Illustration 7.

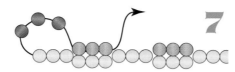

Continue to add groups of three until you reach the hinge. Add two single beads as shown in Illustrations 8 & 9.

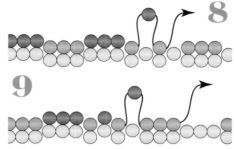

Complete the row with groups of three beads. When you reach the end of the row, reverse direction and add a group of three beads to begin the next row *(Illustration 10)*.

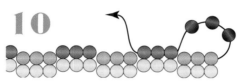

Rows 4 to 23:
Work as you did for row 3, adding groups of three beads until you come to the hinge, work 2 single beads and then complete each row with groups of three.

Let's face facts:
You're going to run out of thread at some point, but there's no need to panic - or to tie a knot! To end a thread, weave up and down through a few bead groups on the rows below. Clip thread end *(Illustration 11)*. Cut a new length of thread and weave up and down through a few bead groups to come up out of the last bead group you added *(Illustration 12)*. Weave down to end a thread, weave up to start a new one.

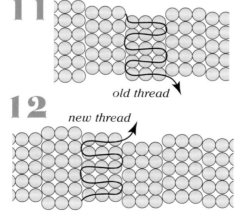

old thread

new thread

Here's a tip to help you determine which row you are working on: count the rows on the diagonal as shown in Illustration 13.

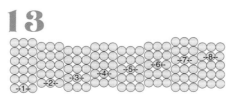

Keep your treasures safe!

Now we'll begin to shape the flap.
Row 24: Begin this row with a decrease as shown in Illustration 14. Work the rest of the row as before.

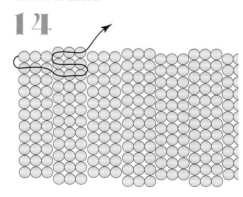

Row 25: Turn and work row 25.
Row 26: Work another beginning decrease as shown in Illustration 15.

last group of row 25

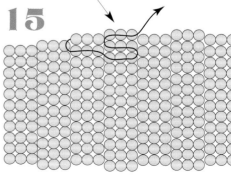

Continued on page 10.

Goddess of Credit

Shaping the Flap

Rows 27 to 37: Work as for rows 25 to 26 decreasing at the beginning of each even numbered row.
Rows 38 to 58: Do not decrease. Turn and work as for rows 3 to 23 *(Illustration 16)*.

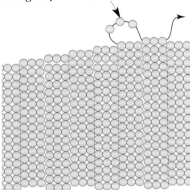

16

first group of row 38

Weave the thread through several bead groups and cut close. Untie the 'stopper' bead from the opposite end of the piece, thread the needle with the 6" tail and weave it through several groups of beads before cutting thread.
Let's stitch the sides of the bag.
Fold the bottom of the bag up so that the bottom row of beads is just below the hinge section (single bead rows). Notice how the edges line up just like a zipper? You're going to stitch the zipper closed by running a thread through the bead groups on the sides of the bag as shown in Illustration 17. Secure the ends of the thread through several groups of beads before clipping.

17

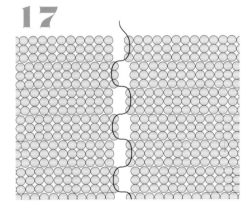

Make and Attach Pendant

Each turquoise button is slightly different in size. You may have to adjust the number of seed beads in these diagrams to accommodate your own pendant.

Thread the needle with 36" of thread. Pass the thread through the Turquoise button and then string the Brass disk and about 14 seed beads. Tie a knot *(Illustration 18)*.
Thread another 14 seed beads and pass the needle back through the center holes of the brass disk and the button. Tie another knot *(Illustration 19)*.

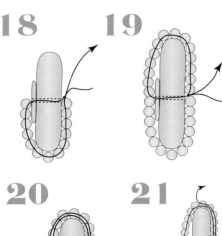

18   **19**

20   **21**

Pass the thread through all the beads, making a loop around the button. Bring the needle out at the bottom of the loop as shown in Illustration 20.
Thread on two seed beads, the goddess and two more seed beads. Pass the needle back through all the beads and the pendant one more time as shown in Illustration 21. Bring the needle out at the top of the loop as shown.

Now stitch completed pendant to the front flap. Bring the needle up through the sixth group of beads from the right edge. Pass the needle down through the next group to the right (fifth from the edge). Bring the needle back through the center bead of the loop from *back to front* as shown in Illustration 22.

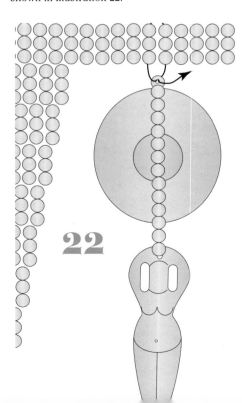

22

Repeat the process in reverse: Bring the needle up through the fifth group of beads from the right edge. Pass the needle down through the next group to the left (sixth from the edge). Bring the needle back through the center bead of the loop from *back to front* as shown in Illustration 23.

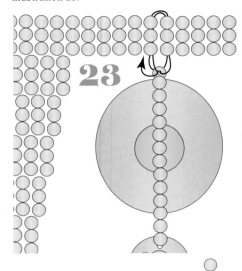

23

We won't need a needle for the strap. Insert one end of the beading wire down through the group at one corner of the bag. Weave the wire end through a few groups as shown in Illustration 24.

Thread the beads for the strap as shown in the illustration at right. Reverse the beading pattern at the opposite side and take the beading wire down through the top of the group at the other corner. Secure the end by weaving it through a few groups *(Illustration 24)*.
Clip the beading wire.

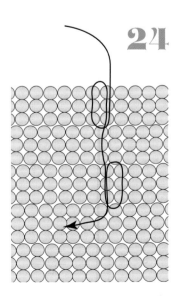

24

Samples made by Bonnie Brooks and Ida Williams

*Make a home for your
'most treasured' possession...
the goddess will guard your wealth!*

Diva Pendant Hourglass

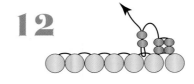

Finished size: approximately 1¼" x 3½"

General Materials

Bead for head • Disk bead for neck • Assorted beads for arms and legs • Bead for hanging loop • Drops or charms for hands and feet • Beading thread and needle

Purple & Blue Diva
Toho Beads:
2 grams 11/0 #461 • 2 grams 11/0 #942 • 4 grams of 6/0 #942

Red Diva
Toho Beads:
3 grams 11/0 #5 • 1 gram 11/0 #5B • 4 grams 6/0 #5BF

Gold Diva
Toho Beads:
3 grams 11/0 #103 • 1 gram 11/0 #6CF • 4 grams 6/0 #222

1

See beading chart on page 14 for bead colors
Row 1: Thread your needle with 48" of thread. Make an overhand knot around a 6/0 bead about 12" from the end as shown in Illustration 1. Be sure to leave a 12" tail. We'll be needing it very soon…

2

Next we'll make a ladder. If you haven't used this method before it may help to lay your work out on a table until you get used to it. Thread on 7 size 6/0 beads. Move them down to within a few inches of the stopper bead. Take your needle back through the 2nd bead from the end as shown in Illustration 2. Pull your thread slowly. (The bead on the end will turn over.)

Arrange the beads as shown in Illustration 3.
Pass your needle back through the next bead as shown in Illustration 4. Pull your thread slowly. (The set of two beads will turn over.)
Arrange the beads as shown in Illustration 5.

Pass your needle back through the next bead as shown in Illustration 6. Pull your thread slowly. (The set of 3 beads will turn over.) Arrange the beads as shown in Illustration 7.
Continue in this manner until all 7 beads have been added to the ladder. You may have to move the stopper bead farther down the tail from time to time as this method uses thread from both ends.
Row 2: Position the ladder as shown in Illustration 8.

3

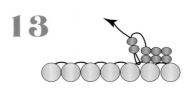

4

5

6

7

8

String four 11/0 beads. Notice the loops connecting each group of beads across the top edge of Row 1. Hook the needle under the first loop. Bring the needle back up through the last two beads (Illustration 9).

9

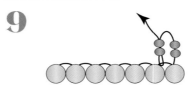

Pass the needle back down through the first set of beads and then back up through the second set (Illustrations 10 & 11). This 'locks' the first group of beads to the second and keeps it in line with the rest of the row.

10

11

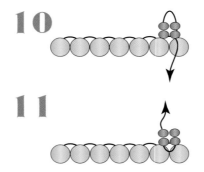

String two beads, hook needle under next loop and bring needle back up through beads (Illustration 12).

12

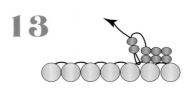

Work a second set of 11/0 beads in the same loop (Illustration 13).

13

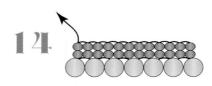

Continue to work two sets of size 11/0 beads over each of the loops of Row 1. You should have 12 groups of 11/0 beads in this row (Illustration 14).

14

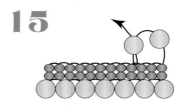

Row 3: Thread on 2 size 6/0 beads. Skip the first two loops and hook the needle under the third loop. Bring needle back up through the last size 6/0 seed bead (Illustration 15).

15

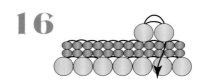

Pass the needle back down through the first 6/0 bead and then back up through the second (Illustrations 16 & 17). This 'locks' the first bead to the second and keeps it in line with the rest of the row.

16

17

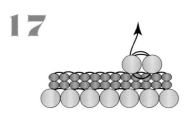

Thread another big seed bead. Hook needle under second loop from last stitch and bring needle back up through the same bead *(Illustration 18)*.

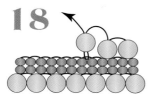

Finish the row. You should have 6 size 6/0 beads in Row 3.

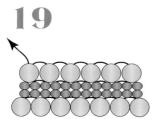

Row 4: Work as for Row 2 *(Illustration 20)*.

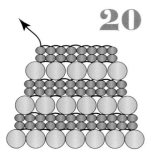

Row 5: Work as for Row 3 *(Illustration 21)*.

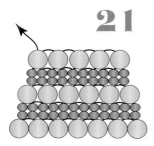

Row 6: Work as for Row 2 *(Illustration 22)*.

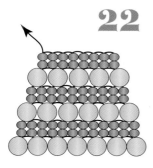

Row 7: Work as for Row 3 *(Illustration 23)*.

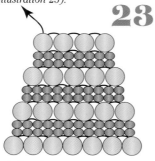

Let's face facts:
You're going to run out of thread at some point, but there's no need to panic - or to tie a knot! To end a thread, weave down through several bead groups on the rows below. Clip thread end. Cut another 36" length of thread and weave up through several bead groups on the rows below to come up out of the last group of beads you added. Weave down to end a thread, weave up to start a new one *(Illustration 24)*.

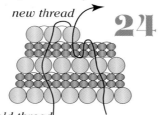
new thread
old thread

Weave the end of thread through several rows of stitching to secure. Clip close.
Remove the stopper bead and secure the tail the same way.
Make another triangle just as you did for this piece, but only work through Row 6.
Turn the first triangle over and join the two pieces as shown in Illustration 25.
Weave the end of thread through several rows of stitching to secure. Clip close.

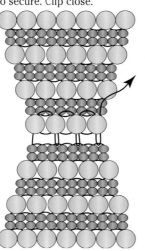

Continued on page 14.
Samples made by Dale Leuthold and Melinda Boldt

These little beauties, dressed in beaded costumes, will grace any outfit, or hang one in a window to lure good fortune your way!

Diva Pendant

Continued from page 13.

Attaching Arms & Legs

Attach the arm and leg pieces as shown in Illustrations 26 & 27.

It isn't necessary to have the exact beads as the examples. Play around with the beads you have on hand. Use drops or charms for the hands and feet.

To attach the head bead, follow the thread path shown in Illustration 28.

Make several passes through the beads to secure the head well. Weave the end of the thread through several rows of stitching before clipping close.

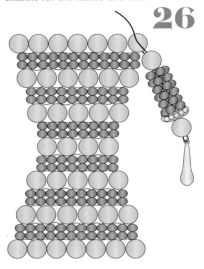

26

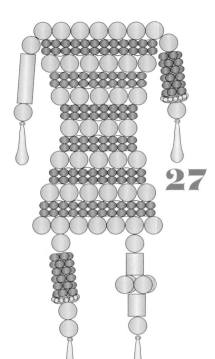

27

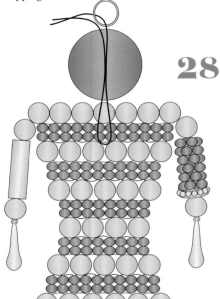

28

Beading Patterns

Blue & Purple Diva

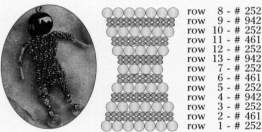

row 8 - # 252	
row 9 - # 942	
row 10 - # 252	
row 11 - # 461	
row 12 - # 252	
row 13 - # 942	
row 7 - # 252	
row 6 - # 461	
row 5 - # 252	
row 4 - # 942	
row 3 - # 252	
row 2 - # 461	
row 1 - # 252	

Red Diva

row 8 - # 5BF	
row 9 - # 5	
row 10 - # 5BF	
row 11 - # 5	
row 12 - # 5BF	
row 13 - # 5	
row 7 - # 5BF	
row 6 - # 5	
row 5 - # 5BF	
row 4 - # 5	
row 3 - # 5BF	
row 2 - # 5	
row 1 - # 5BF	

Gold & Bronze Diva

row 8 - # 222	
row 9 - # 2C	
row 10 - # 222	
row 11 - # 2C	
row 12 - # 222	
row 13 - # 2C	
row 7 - # 222	
row 6 - # 2C	
row 5 - # 222	
row 4 - # 2C	
row 3 - # 222	
row 2 - # 2C	
row 1 - # 222	

How to Make the Beaded Arm and Leg Pieces

To make the beaded arm and leg pieces we are going to switch to peyote stitch. Begin by threading 6 11/0 beads onto a 36" length of thread.

Pick up another bead. Take your needle through the second bead from the end.

Pick up another bead. Skip the next bead and pass your needle through the second bead.

Pick up another bead. Skip the next bead and pass your needle through the second bead.

Notice how the new beads share the space with the beads from the original row?

Pick up a bead. Pass your needle through the first 'high' bead of the row.

Pick up a bead. Pass your needle through the next 'high' bead of the row.

Add the last bead of the row the same way.

Work a total of 8 rows in this manner.

Fold the piece in half lengthwise. You see the edges fit together like the teeth of a zipper. Stitch the teeth together as shown above. The Illustration shows you the thread path only - you'll tighten your thread and form the piece into a tube.

Tie the ends together and then weave the ends through several rows of stitching to secure before clipping close.

Beaded Knee Piece

To make the beaded 'knee' piece, begin with a 4 bead ladder just as you did for the body.

Join the first bead to the last.

Tie the ends together to secure.

Doll is 3¾" x 5¾"

General Materials:

⅛" plastic tube or dowel • 2 Worldly Goods hand charms # C702YB • Beading thread and needle • Polyester fiberfill
White and Bronze Doll Toho beads:
40 grams 11/0 #763 • 8 grams 11/0 #514F
Black and Green Doll Toho beads:
40 grams 11/0 #610 • 8 grams 11/0 #561

Let's begin: The First Half

Rows 1 to 2: Pour a few beads of each color into a small shallow bowl or beading tray. Cut a 48" length of thread, thread the needle with one end. Make an overhand

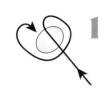

knot around a bead about 12" from the end as shown in Illustration 1. Be sure to leave a 6" tail.
Thread on the following:
18 light, 8 dark, 4 light, 2 dark, 8 light and 56 dark beads.
Row 3: Pick up two more dark beads and pass the needle back through the second pair of beads from the end *(Illustration 2).*
This project is worked in 2 drop peyote stitch - we'll always be working with pairs of beads.

Add two more beads as shown in Illustration 3.

Add two more beads *(Illustration 4).*
Notice how the beads from the first row 'share' the space with the new beads?

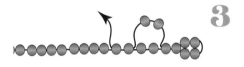

Add 11 more pairs of dark beads in this manner. Then add 2 pairs of light beads, 1 pair of dark beads, 1 pair of light beads, 2 pairs of dark beads and 4 pairs of light beads.

Row 4: When you reach the end of Row 3, reverse direction and add the first pair of Row 4 as shown in Illustration 5 (light beads).

Stitch the remaining beads as shown in Illustration 6.

Refer to the beading pattern or the word chart to complete the row.
Row 4 (l to r): 7L 2D 15L **means**
Row 4 is worked from left to right. You stitch 7 light, 2 dark and 15 light pairs of beads to complete the row.

Rows 5 to 9: Refer to the beading pattern and/or the word chart to complete these rows.

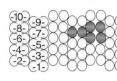

Here's a tip to help you determine which row you are on: count the rows along the edge as shown in Illustration 7.

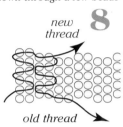

You're going to run out of thread at some point, but there's no need to panic - or to tie a knot! To end a thread, weave down through a few beads on the rows below and clip the end. Weave the new thread up through a few beads to come up out of the last bead you added. Weave down to end a thread, weave up to start a new one *(Illustration 8).*

new thread

old thread

OK, now that all of THAT is out of the way, let's bead!
We were just about to begin Row 10…
Row 10: Working from left to right, stitch 4 pairs of light beads.
At this point, we are going to concentrate on stitching just the head of the doll - we'll pick up where we left off on the body in just a bit.
Row 11: Follow the thread path shown in Illustration 9 to begin the row.

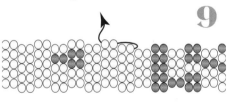

Stitch 3 pairs of light beads to complete the row *(Illustration 10).*

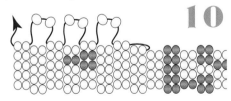

Row 12: Stitch 3 pair of light beads.
Row 13: Follow the thread path shown in Illustration 11 to begin Row 13 (head).

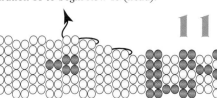

Stitch 2 pairs of light beads to complete the row *(Illustration 12).*

Row 14: Follow the thread path shown in Illustration 13 to work Row 14 (head) and prepare to work Row 10 (body).

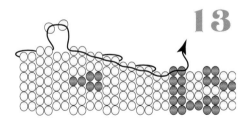

Row 10: (body) The first stitch of the row is shown in Illustration 14. Refer to the beading pattern and the word chart to complete the row.

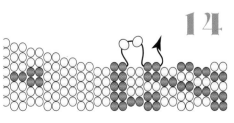

Continued on page 16.

Continued from page 15.

Beading Patterns & Charts

First Half of Front

body
Rows 1 and 2: **beads** 18L 8D 4L 2D 8L 56D
Row 3 (r to l): **pairs** 14D 2L 1D 1L 2D 4L
Row 4 (l to r): 7L 2D 15L
Row 5 (r to l): 15L 1D 1L 1D 1L 1D 4L
Row 6 (l to r): 2L 1D 3L 1D 2L 1D 14L
Row 7 (r to l): 16L 1D 1L 2D 2L 1D 1L
Row 8 (l to r): 2L 1D 4L 3D 14L
Row 9 (r to l): 17L 3D 4L

head only
Row 10 (l to r): 4L
Row 11 (r to l): (decrease) 3L
Row 12 (l to r): 3L
Row 13 (r to l): (decrease) 2L
Row 14 (l to r): (decrease) 1L

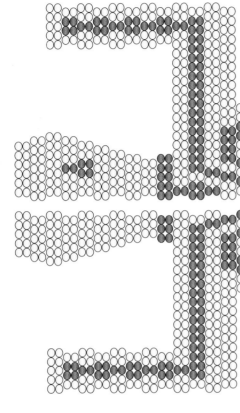

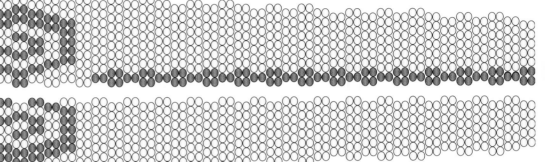

body
Row 10 (l to r): 3L 2D 14L
Row 11 (r to l): 16L 3D
Row 12 (l to r): 4L 1D 14L
Row 13 (r to l): 15L 1D 1L 2D
Row 14 (l to r): 2L 3D 14L
Row 15 (r to l): (decrease) 14L 4D
Row 16 (l to r): 2L 2D 12L
Row 17 (r to l): (decrease) 9L 1D 1L 1D
Row 18 (l to r): 10L
Row 19 (r to l): (decrease) 6L 1D
Row 20 (l to r): 4L
Row 21 (r to l): (decrease) 1L 1D
Row 22 (l to r): 2L
Row 23 (r to l): 1L 1D
Row 24 (l to r): 2L

Row 25 (r to l): 1L 1D
Row 26 (l to r): 2L
Row 27 (r to l): 1L 1D
Row 28 (l to r): 2L
Row 29 (r to l): 1L 1D
Row 30 (l to r): 2L
Row 31 (r to l): 1L 1D
Row 32 (l to r): 2L
Row 33 (r to l): 1L 1D
Row 34 (l to r): 2L
Row 35 (r to l): 1L 1D **beads** 16L
Row 36 (l to r): 6L
Row 37 (r to l): 1L 5D
Row 38 (l to r): 1L 4D 1L
Row 39 (r to l): 1L 5D
Row 40 (l to r): 6L
Row 41 (r to l): 6L
Row 42 (l to r): 6L

Second Half of Front

body
Row 43 (l to r): 7L 2D 15L
Row 44 (r to l): 15L 1D 1L 1D 1L 1D 4L
Row 45 (l to r): 6L 1D 2L 1D 14L
Row 46 (r to l): 16L 1D 1L 2D 4L
Row 47 (l to r): 7L 3D 14L
Row 48 (r to l): 17L 3D 4L

head only
Row 49 (l to r): 4L
Row 50 (r to l): (decrease) 3L
Row 51 (l to r): 3L
Row 52 (r to l): (decrease) 2L
Row 53 (l to r): (decrease) 1L

body
Row 49 (l to r): 3L 2D 14L
Row 50 (r to l): 16L 3D
Row 51 (l to r): 4L 1D 14L
Row 52 (r to l): 15L 1D 1L 2D
Row 53 (l to r): 2L 3D 14L
Row 54 (r to l): (decrease)14L 4D
Row 55 (l to r): 2L 2D 12L
Row 56 (r to l): (decrease) 9L 1D 1L 1D
Row 57 (l to r): 10L
Row 58 (r to l): (decrease) 6L 1D
Row 59 (l to r): 4L
Row 60 (r to l): (decrease) 1L 1D
Row 61 (l to r): 2L
Row 62 (r to l): 1L 1D
Row 63 (l to r): 2L

Row 64 (r to l): 1L 1D
Row 65 (l to r): 2L
Row 66 (r to l): 1L 1D
Row 67 (l to r): 2L
Row 68 (r to l): 1L 1D
Row 69 (l to r): 2L
Row 70 (r to l): 1L 1D
Row 71 (l to r): 2L
Row 72 (r to l): 1L 1D
Row 73 (l to r): 2L
Row 74 (r to l): 1L 1D **beads** 16L
Row 75 (l to r): 6L
Row 76 (r to l): 1L 5D
Row 77 (l to r): 1L 4D 1L
Row 78 (r to l): 1L 5D
Row 79 (l to r): 6L
Row 80 (r to l): 6L
Row 81 (l to r): 6L

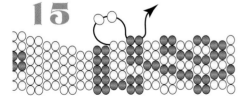

Row 11: (body) Refer to the beading pattern and the word chart to complete the row.
Row 12: (body) Turn and begin the row as shown in Illustration 15. Refer to the beading pattern and the word charts above to complete the row.

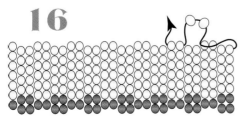

Row 15: Follow the thread path shown in Illustration 16 to begin the row. Refer to the beading pattern and word charts above to complete the row.

Row 16: Refer to the beading pattern and word charts above to complete the row.

Row 17: Follow the thread path shown in Illustration 17 to begin the row. Refer to the beading pattern and word charts above to complete the row.

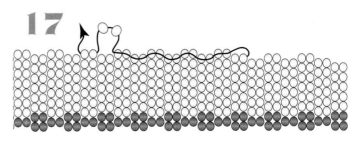

Row 18: Refer to the beading pattern and word charts above to complete the row.

First Half of Back

<u>body</u>
Rows 1 and 2: **beads** 18L 2D 2L 74D
Row 3 (r to l): **pairs** 20D 4L
Row 4 (l to r): 24L
Row 5 (r to l): 18L 2D 4L
Row 6 (l to r): 24L
Row 7 (r to l): 18L 2D 4L
Row 8 (l to r): 24L
Row 9 (r to l): 18L 2D 4L

<u>head only</u>
Row 10 (l to r): 4L
Row 11 (r to l): (decrease) 3L
Row 12 (l to r): 3L
Row 13 (r to l): (decrease) 2L
Row 14 (l to r): (decrease) 1L

<u>body</u>
Row 10 (l to r): 19L
Row 11 (r to l): 18L 1D
Row 12 (l to r): 19L
Row 13 (r to l): 18L 1D
Row 14 (l to r): 19L
Row 15 (r to l): (decrease) 17L 1D
Row 16 (l to r): 16L
Row 17 (r to l): (decrease) 11L 1D
Row 18 (l to r): 10L
Row 19 (r to l): (decrease) 6L 1D
Row 20 (l to r): 4L
Row 21 (r to l): (decrease) 1L 1D
Row 22 (l to r): 2L
Row 23 (r to l): 1L 1D
Row 24 (l to r): 2L
Row 25 (r to l): 1L 1D

Row 26 (l to r): 2L
Row 27 (r to l): 1L 1D
Row 28 (l to r): 2L
Row 29 (r to l): 1L 1D
Row 30 (l to r): 2L
Row 31 (r to l): 1L 1D
Row 32 (l to r): 2L
Row 33 (r to l): 1L 1D
Row 34 (l to r): 2L
Row 35 (r to l): 1L 1D **beads** 16L
Row 36 (l to r): 6L
Row 37 (r to l): 1L 5D
Row 38 (l to r): 1L 4D 1L
Row 39 (r to l): 1L 5D
Row 40 (l to r): 6L
Row 41 (r to l): 6L
Row 42 (l to r): 6L

Second Half of Back

<u>body</u>
Row 43 (l to r): 24L
Row 44 (r to l): 18L 2D 4L
Row 45 (l to r): 24L
Row 46 (r to l): 18L 2D 4L
Row 47 (l to r): 24L
Row 48 (r to l): 18L 2D 4L

<u>head only</u>
Row 49 (l to r): 4L
Row 50 (r to l): (decrease) 3L
Row 51 (l to r): 3L
Row 52 (r to l): (decrease) 2L
Row 53 (l to r): (decrease) 1L

<u>body</u>
Row 49 (l to r): 19L
Row 50 (r to l): 18L 1D
Row 51 (l to r): 19L
Row 52 (r to l): 18L 1D
Row 53 (l to r): 19L
Row 54 (r to l): (decrease) 17L 1D
Row 55 (l to r): 16L
Row 56 (r to l): (decrease) 11L 1D
Row 57 (l to r): 10L
Row 58 (r to l): (decrease) 6L 1D
Row 59 (l to r): 4L
Row 60 (r to l): (decrease) 1L 1D
Row 61 (l to r): 2L
Row 62 (r to l): 1L 1D
Row 63 (l to r): 2L
Row 64 (r to l): 1L 1D

Row 65 (l to r): 2L
Row 66 (r to l): 1L 1D
Row 67 (l to r): 2L
Row 68 (r to l): 1L 1D
Row 69 (l to r): 2L
Row 70 (r to l): 1L 1D
Row 71 (l to r): 2L
Row 72 (r to l): 1L 1D
Row 73 (l to r): 2L
Row 74 (r to l): 1L 1D **beads** 16L
Row 75 (l to r): 6L
Row 76 (r to l): 1L 5D
Row 77 (l to r): 1L 4D 1L
Row 78 (r to l): 1L 5D
Row 79 (l to r): 6L
Row 80 (r to l): 6L
Row 81 (l to r): 6L

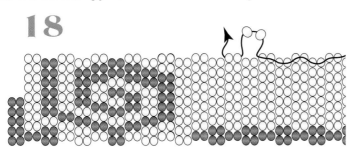

Row 19: Follow the thread path shown in Illustration 18 to begin the row. Refer to the beading pattern and word charts to complete the row.

18

Row 20: Refer to the beading pattern and word charts to complete the row.
Row 21: Follow the thread path shown in Illustration 19 to begin the row. Refer to the beading pattern and word charts to complete the row.

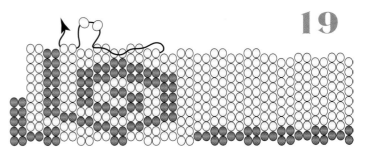

19

Rows 22 to 34: Refer to the beading pattern and word charts to complete these rows.
Row 35: Work 11L 1D, then pick up 16 light beads.

20

Row 36: Turn and work the 16 beads as you did for Rows 1 & 2 *(Illustration 20)*.

Continued on page 18.

Continued from page 17.

The First Half

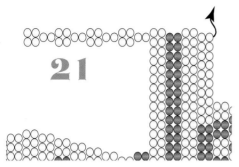

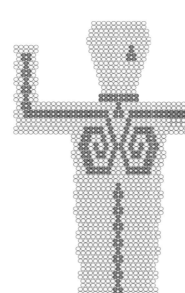

Complete the row as shown in Illustration 21.

Rows 35 to 42: Refer to the beading pattern and word charts to complete these rows. Weave the thread through several rows of stitching to secure before clipping close. Remove the stopper bead from the beginning of the piece and weave in it as well.

Take a little break. Stretch your legs. Have a cup of tea. Don't worry, we'll wait for you.

Let's Begin the Second Half

Rows 43 to 81: To this point, the beading diagrams and word charts have been oriented from the bottom up. With this half of the piece they will reference beads from the top down. You will begin stitching this row at the lower left of the head. This side is almost a mirror image of the first (with the exception of the 'eye'). The decreases are exactly the same as before. You may want to turn your piece over so that you can reference the illustrations given for the first half.

Let's Stitch the Back
Now that you've done the front, the back ought to be a piece of cake! Refer to the beading pattern, word charts and previous illustrations to help you along. The thread paths for the decrease in the head and body are the same for the back piece as they were for the front.

Please Note: The beads shaded in gray on this side of the doll are to be added *after* the entire piece is completed. The easiest way to do this is to run your thread along the outside edge of the back piece and add the beads where they are indicated on the beading pattern. These beads aid in stitching the front and back pieces together. Which brings us to...

Stitching the front and back together.
This is a good time to remember that beading is an art - not a science! Sometimes you have to use your imagination to get the job done. When you line up the two halves of your doll you will notice that sometimes the sides match up like the teeth of a zipper and sometimes they are mirror images of each other. Illustration 22 will give you some idea as to how to stitch these lovely bits together.

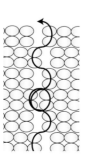

Whipstitch the loops across the top and bottom of the arm section. Stuff the head lightly before whipstitching the top together. Stuff the body lightly before whipstitching the bottom loops. Don't stuff the arm section. Instead, insert a length of 1/8" wood dowel rod before stitching closed. *(Illustration 23)*

Hands: To tack the hands in place, run your thread through several stitches near the bottom of the arm. Run your thread up through the hollow tube that forms the forearm of the doll and catch the loop of the hand charm. Run your thread back down through the forearm tube and pull the hand gently into place. Secure by running thread through several stitches and clipping close.

Hair: The hair is made by alternating strands of twisted and branch fringe. The illustrations provided here are only guidelines. Make your doll's hair as long, short or wild as you like. You'll make two rows of hair which are stitched to the two rows of beading across the top of the doll head.

Making Fringe for Hair

To make branch fringe:
Bring your thread out of one of the beads at the top of the doll's head. Thread on several beads. Skip the last bead in the row and pass your needle back up through a few beads.
Thread on beads for the first branch. Skip the last bead. Take your needle back through the rest of the branch beads and up a few more beads of the original row.
Continue making branches to the end of the original row. Pass your needle back through the bead where you started *(Illustration 24)*.

To make the twisted fringe:
Bring your thread out of one of the beads at the top of the doll's head. Thread on several beads. Grasp the thread near the last bead between your thumb and forefinger. Let your needle dangle. Twist the beading thread several times until the bead strand starts to twist upon itself. Arrange the twists with your free hand and then pass your needle back through the bead where you started *(Illustration 25)*.

Samples made by Anne Tisdale

Take doll making in a new direction when your make this beaded version! Make her in one of our color combinations or choose your two favorite colors.

Finished size is 6" long

General Materials

Cord for hanging • Three face beads • 6 small disk beads • Beading thread and needle

Tan Tassel
Toho Beads:
26 grams 11/0 #551F • 8 grams 11/0 #514 • 5 grams 11/0 #558F • 4 grams 11/0 #763 • 5 grams 6/0 #221 • 3 grams #3 bugle #221

Black Tassel
Toho Beads:
36 grams 11/0 #610 • 6 grams 11/0 #558 • 2 grams 11/0 #221 • 2 grams 11/0 #222 • 5 grams 6/0 #222 • 3 grams #3 bugle #221

Crystal Tassel
Toho Beads:
39 grams 11/0 #21F • 5 grams 11/0 #101 • 4 grams 11/0 #1 • 5 grams 6/0 #21 • 3 grams #3 bugle #21

Note: Step-by-step instructions are given for the Tan Tassel. Refer to the beading patterns on page 23 for the Black and Crystal versions.

The BIG Picture

Here's an overview of how the tassel will be made: first we are going to make a tube for the hanging cord. Next we'll attach the head of the tassel which will be made in one long continuous piece. We'll make four decreases along its top edge and add fringe to the bottom edge. Then we'll roll the headpiece around the tube and 'zip up' the seam.

Let's Begin

1

Rows 1 to 2: Pour a few beads into a small shallow bowl or beading tray. Cut a 48" length of thread, thread the needle with one end. Make an overhand knot around a bead about 6" from the end as shown in Illustration 1. Be sure to leave a 6" tail.

String 32 beads on the thread.
Pick up two more beads and pass the needle back through the second pair of beads from the end. This project is worked in 2 drop peyote stitch - we'll always be working with pairs of beads *(Illustration 2)*.

2

Add two more beads as shown in Illustration 3.

3

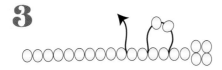

Notice how the beads from the first row 'share' the space with the new beads? Add a total of 8 groups along the first row. Try to adjust your tension so that the row looks like Illustration 4.

4

When you reach the end of the row, reverse direction and add the first pair of the next row as shown in Illustration 5.

5

Continue to add pairs of beads to the end of the row as shown in Illustration 6.

6

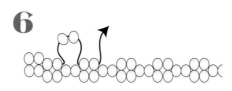

Reverse direction and continue to add a total of 20 rows to your piece. The finished piece should look like Illustration 7.

7

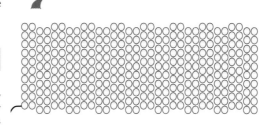

While we are on the subject...

Here's a tip to help you determine which row you are working on: count the rows on the diagonal as shown in Illustration 8.

8

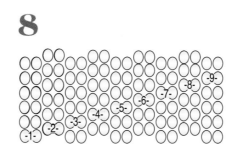

You're going to run out of thread at some point, but there's no need to panic - or to tie a knot! To end a thread, weave down through a few beads on the rows below and clip the end. Weave the new thread up through a few beads to come up out of the last bead you added. Weave down to end a thread, weave up to start a new one *(Illustration 9)*.

9

weave up to start a new thread

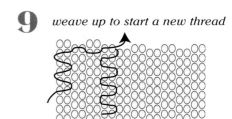

weave down to end an old thread

Now we are going to zip up the tube for the hanging cord. First, remove the stopper bead.
Fold the piece in half lengthwise. You see the edges fit together like the teeth of a zipper. Stitch the teeth together as shown in Illustration 10. The illustration shows you the thread path only - you'll tighten your thread and form the piece into a tube of course! Your finished tube should look like Illustration 11.

10

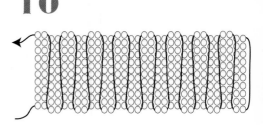

11

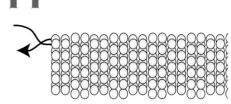

Tie the end of the thread and the tail together securely.

Tassel Head:
Row 1: String two beads and pass through the second pair of beads on the nearest row of the tube *(Illustration 12)*.

12

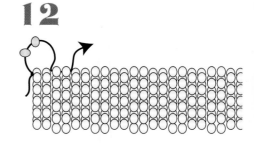

When you have added 7 pairs of beads along the row, reverse direction and begin Row 2. This is the first of our three decreases *(Illustrations 13 & 14)*.

Continued on page 22.

Samples made by Frieda Bates, Marilou Porth and Vicki Mollinar-Stevens

*Turn a beautiful
'face' to the world.
Beaded tassels are
great accents to
hang on lamps,
drawer pulls and
draperies!*

Continued from page 9.

Making the Tassel Head

13

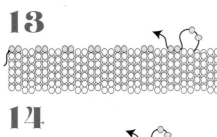

14

Stitch a total of 32 rows.
Turn and begin the next row with a pair of beads as shown in Illustration 15.

15

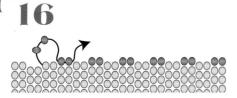

Work 6 pairs of beads for this row. Then turn and work in the opposite direction. Second decrease completed *(Illustration 16)*. Work a total of 46 rows.

16

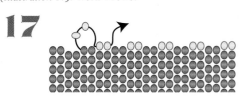

Begin the next row with a pair of beads. Work only five pairs of beads for this row before turning and working in the opposite direction. Third decrease completed *(Illustration 17)*. Work 4 rows.

17

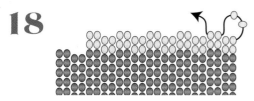

Now we are going to stitch the windows for our goddess charms. First we'll work the right half...
Row 5 (right side): Turn and work one pair of beads *(Illustration 18)*.

18

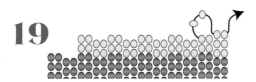

Row 6: Turn and work one pair of beads *(Illustration 19)*.

19

Rows 7 to 18 (right side): Turn and work one pair of beads in each row. Weave thread back down to Row 4 and bring needle out of beads indicated in Illustration 20.

20

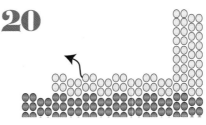

Row 5 (left side): Turn and work one pair of beads as shown in Illustration 21.

21

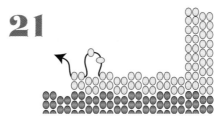

Rows 6 to 18 (left side): Turn and work one pair of beads for each row. At the end of Row 18 thread on 12 beads and thread your needle through both bead groups on the right side as shown in Illustration 22.

22

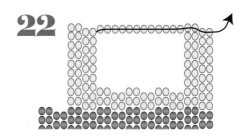

Row 19: Turn and work across the row. Work the center 12 beads just as you did for Row 3 *(Illustration 23)*.

23

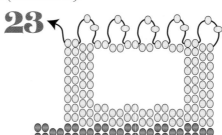

Rows 20 to 24: Turn and work 5 bead groups across each row *(Illustration 24)*.

24

Rows 25 to 38 (right side): Work one pair of beads per row as for Rows 5 to 18. (right side)
Rows 25 to 38 (left side): Work one pair of beads per row as for Rows 5 to 18 (left side).

Continued on page 24.

Rows 39 to 44: Work as for Rows 20 to 24.
Rows 45 to 58 (right side): Work one pair of beads per row as for Rows 5 to 18 (right side).
Rows 45 to 58 (left side): Work one pair of beads per row as for Rows 5 to 18 (left side).
Row 59 to 60: Work 5 pairs of beads across each row.

The beading patterns show the completed piece for each color version.

Tan Tassel

○ 11/0 # 763
◎ 11/0 # 551F
● 11/0 # 514F
○ 11/0 # 558F
◯ 6/0 # 221
▬ #3 bugle #221

Make your own fabulous tassels at home !

Black Tassel

- 11/0 # 610
- 11/0 # 221
- 11/0 # 558
- 11/0 # 222
- 6/0 # 222
- #3 bugle #221

Crystal Tassel

- 11/0 # 21F
- 11/0 # 101
- 11/0 # 1
- 6/0 # 21
- #3 bugle #21

Beautiful Tassels

Finishing the Tassel

25 Stitch the Goddesses in place.
Stitch a disk bead, a face bead and another disk bead in the center of each window as shown in Illustration 25.

Let's add the fringe!
Your thread should be coming out of the bottom of the tassel head. Thread 17 seed beads, a #3 bugle, 3 seed beads, a 6/0 bead and another 11/0 bead. This last bead is called the turning bead. It's the bead that holds the strand in place. Pass the needle back up through all the beads except the turning bead *(Illustration 26)*.

Take your needle up through the last pair of beads on the tassel head and then back down through the pair just to the left *(Illustration 27)*.

Continue adding fringe in this manner until you reach the end of the section (30 rows). See Illustration 28 for bead and row counts of remaining fringe.

26 27

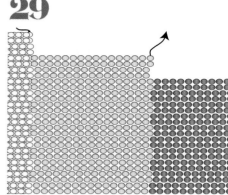

Weave the end of your thread through several stitches to secure before clipping. Begin a new piece of thread 24" long. Weave the end through several rows of stitching before finally emerging at the top of the first decrease as shown in Illustration 29.

29

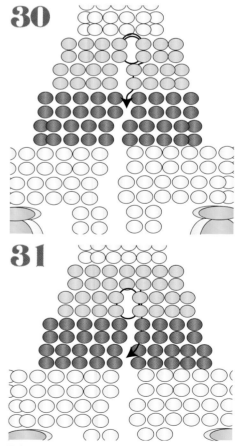

Ready for the fun part?
Carefully roll the long tassel head around the tube. (You may find a chopstick or small dowel helpful for this step.)
Notice how the ends of the sections fit together like a zipper? Our next step is to stitch those ends together as shown in Illustrations 30 & 31. The illustrations show you how to stitch the first section together. Stitch the rest of the sections together in the same manner.

28

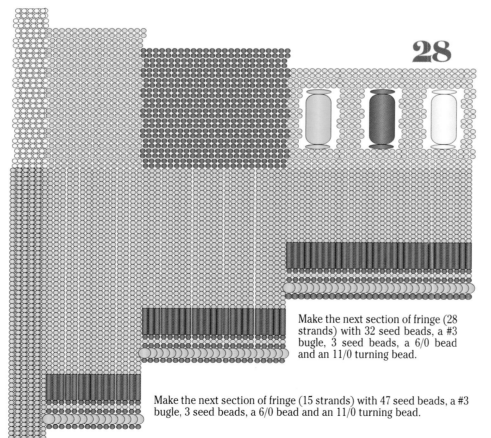

Make the next section of fringe (28 strands) with 32 seed beads, a #3 bugle, 3 seed beads, a 6/0 bead and an 11/0 turning bead.

Make the next section of fringe (15 strands) with 47 seed beads, a #3 bugle, 3 seed beads, a 6/0 bead and an 11/0 turning bead.

The next section of fringe is attached to the original tube (10 strands) with 62 seed beads, a #3 bugle, 3 seed beads, a 6/0 bead and an 11/0 turning bead.

30

31

Fold the hanging cord in half and thread the looped end up through the bottom of the tassel - try threading a doubled piece of beading thread through the loop first, thread the ends of the beading thread through the tassel and pull the cord up after it.

Finished size varies with gourd used.

General Materials

Gourd • Assortment of beads and charms • Jig saw or Dremel tool • Beading thread and needle • Drill and 1/16" drill bit

Red Bowl
Red leather dye
Toho Beads:
6/0 #610 • 6/0 #221 • 11/0 #610 • 11/0 #221
Green Bowl
Purple leather dye (yes, Purple dye!)
Toho Beads:
6/0 #702 • 6/0 #222 • 11/0 #702 • 11/0 #222
Tan Bowl
Tan leather dye
Toho Beads:
6/0 #703 • 6/0 #222 • 11/0 #703 • 11/0 #222

The Gourd

Mark a cut line around the gourd. One easy way to do this is to find a bowl or glass that fits over the top of the gourd. Trace around the lip of the bowl with a pencil.
Cut the top off the gourd with a jig saw or Dremel tool with a cutting blade. Please be careful. Wear eye protection and a dust mask and observe all safety rules when using hand tools.
Clean the inside of the gourd with a spoon. Clip the nipple from the center bottom with wire cutters. You may wish to sand the interior of the gourd for a very clean, smooth look.
Stain the interior and exterior with leather dye. Allow to dry. You may also add a coat of Clear varnish if you wish.

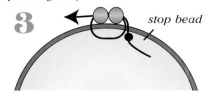

Scribe or mark a line 3/8" from the cut edge of the gourd. You can make a handy tool to help you by taping a couple of pencils together as shown in Illustration 1.

Drill a 1/16" hole every 1/4" along the line you just marked.
For gourds with thinner walls you can burn a hole using a heated awl or ice pick
(Illustration 2).

Cut a 36" long piece of beading thread. Thread the beading needle with one end. Tie a 'stop bead' to the other end. Pick up two size 6/0 seed beads and stitch them to the gourd between two holes as shown in Illustration 3. (The illustration shows the view looking down from above the top of the gourd.)

stop bead

Pick up two more seed beads and stitch them between the last hole worked and the next one in line *(Illustration 4)*.
It may become necessary at times to stitch only one bead as shown in Illustration 5. Stitch these beads very loosely.

Continue stitching until the row of beads extends around the gourd. The only requirement is that you have an even number of beads. If you end up with an odd number, simply remove the last bead.
Pass your needle back through the first bead stitched. Thread on a bead. Skip the next bead in the row and pass your needle through the second bead. Thread on another bead, skip the next bead in the row and thread the needle through the second bead. Repeat the process around the gourd *(Illustration 6)*.

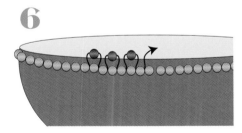

Notice how the beads from the original circle 'share' the space with the new beads? Try to adjust your tension so that the row looks more or less like Illustration 7.

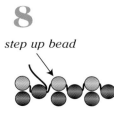

step up bead

Do you see where your thread has come out of the last bead of Row 2? It's smack dab against the first bead of Row 2. This first bead is called the 'step up' bead *(Illustration 8)*.

A gorgeous beauty is born!

step up bead

You have to 'step up' through this bead to begin the next row *(Illustration 9)*. You'll begin every row this way. As you can see, the beads from Row 2 are higher than the rest. In Row 3 we'll place a bead in between each of these higher ones. Thread on a bead and pass your needle through the next high bead
Continue adding beads in this manner to the end of the row *(Illustration 10)*.

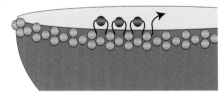

Rows 4 to ??: Step up at the beginning of each row, then add a bead between each of the beads from the previous row.

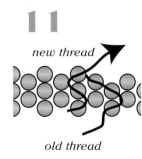

new thread

old thread

Let's face facts:
You're going to run out of thread at some point, but there's no need to panic - or to tie a knot! To end a thread, weave up and down through a few beads on the rows below. Clip thread end. Cut a 36" length of thread and weave up and down through a few beads to come up out of the last bead you added. Weave down to end a thread, weave up to start a new one *(Illustration 11)*.

Continued on page 26.

Continued from page 25.

Beading the Gourd

Continue adding rows until your beadwork extends at least one row over the lip of the gourd *(Illustration 12)*. If your gourd has a 6" opening or larger, continue to stitch another inch above the lip of the gourd.

12

At this point you should be able to fold the beadwork down and against the inside wall of the gourd. Tack the beadwork down with a few stitches from front to back through the holes you drilled in the gourd. Weave your thread back through to the outside bottom edge as shown in Illustration 13.

13

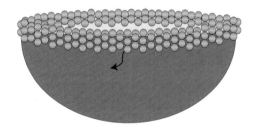

If your gourd has a smaller opening, you will have to decrease evenly around the rim in order to fold the beadwork over to the inside.
To decrease: Stitch seven beads of the next row. Make a stitch without a bead.
Continue in this manner around the rim of the gourd *(Illustrations 14 & 15)*.

14

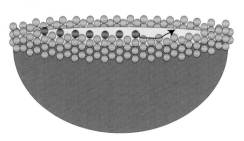

15

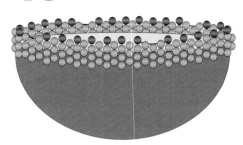

Stitch another row as before, adding a bead between each of the high beads of the previous row as shown in Illustration 16.

16

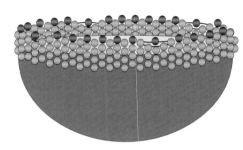

It may be necessary to complete two or three decrease rows depending on the size and shape of the gourd opening.
Tack the beadwork down with a few stitches from front to back through the holes you drilled in the gourd. Weave your thread back through to the outside bottom edge as shown in Illustration 13.

Fringe: Now instead of adding a bead between each of the beads of the previous row, we'll be adding a strand of fringe. Thread on the number of beads you wish for the strand, then add a size 11/0 seed bead or a charm. Skip the last seed bead or charm and pass your needle back through all the beads in the strand. Pass your needle through the next high bead of the previous row of stitching *(Illustration 17)*.
Repeat for each strand.
This is where you can really have some fun and make fringe with all those bits and bobs you've been saving!

17

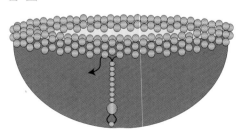

Use your imagination when stitching beads around the rim and adding fringe. The instructions given are for the basic gourd and fringe. Let the samples inspire you to try different types of patterns and fringe on your own gourd.

Samples made by Dana Hall and Valerie Felps

*Turn ordinary gourds
into works of art... cover the
edges with beaded collars
and add colorful fringe!*

Goddess Bracelet

Samples made by Victoria Wilson & Chris Pratt

Finished size: ⅜" wide

General Materials

Two 6mm disk beads • Beading thread • Beading needle

Teal & White Bracelet
Toho Beads:
10 grams treasure #7BD (M) • 4 grams treasure #122 (G) • 2 grams treasure #610 (B)

White & Rose Bracelet
Toho Beads:
10 grams treasure #761 (M) • 4 grams treasure #764 (G) • 2 grams treasure #763 (B)

White & Blue Bracelet
Toho Beads:
7.5 grams 15/0 #A21 (M) • 3 grams 15/0 #A917 (G) • 1.5 grams 15/0 #A22 (B)

Rows 1 to 2: Pour a few beads into a small shallow bowl or beading tray. Cut a 48" length of thread; thread the needle with one end. Thread 2 border color (B), 24 main color (M) and 2 border color (B) beads onto it and slide them down to within 6" of the other end.

Row 3: Add 1B bead as shown in Illustration 1.

Thread on a main color bead. Skip the next bead and pass your needle through the second bead in the row *(Illustration 2)*.

Stitch 11 more main color beads and 1 border bead to complete the row as shown in Illustration 3.

Notice how the beads from the first row 'share' the space with the new beads?

Row 4: Reverse direction.
Add the first bead of the row as shown in Illustration 4. Refer to the beading pattern and word chart to complete the row.
Row 4 (l to r): 1B 12M 1B **means**
Row 4 is worked from left to right. You'll stitch 1 border, 12 main and 1 border color bead to complete the row.

Rows 5 to ??: Refer to the beading pattern and word chart to complete these rows.

Let's face facts:
You're going to run out of thread at some point, but there's no need to panic - or to tie a knot! To end a thread, weave up and down through a few beads on the rows below. Clip thread end. Cut another 36" length of thread and weave up and down through a few beads to come up out of the last bead you added. Weave down to end a thread, weave up to start a new one *(Illustration 5)*.

weave up through several rows to begin a new thread

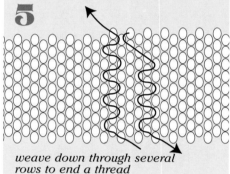

weave down through several rows to end a thread

Thread the needle with the beginning 6" tail of thread and weave it through several rows of stitching to secure. Clip thread close.

A note about length: The pattern as shown yields a bracelet 6¾" long. To make a larger bracelet simply add more rows to each end.

Let's make the loops. Thread needle with 36" of thread and weave it through several rows of stitching, eventually bringing the needle out through the bead shaded in yellow on the far left of Illustration 6. This is where we will make the first bead loop.

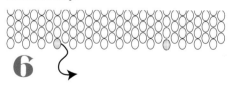

String 13 to 15 main color beads and bring the needle back through the left side of the gray bead as shown in Illustration 7. Weave the needle through the last row of beads until you reach the second yellow bead.

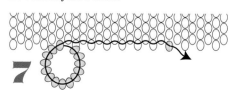

String 13 to 15 main color beads and bring the needle back through the left side of the shaded bead as shown in Illustration 8. Weave the end of thread through several rows of stitching to secure. Clip thread close.

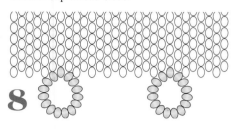

Now we'll add the buttons. Weave a new thread through several rows of stitching to secure, bringing the needle out through the bead shaded in gray on the far left of Illustration 9. This is where we will add the first button.

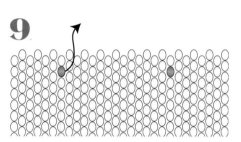

Thread a main color bead, a black disk bead and another main color bead on needle. Pass the needle back through the disk and the first main color bead as shown in Illustration 10. Thread the needle back through the left side of the blue bead as shown. Pull gently on the beads to bring them close to the rows of stitching. Not too close though, you'll need some play in order for the bead loop to hook under it.

It is a good idea to go back through all the button beads a time or two to reinforce them.

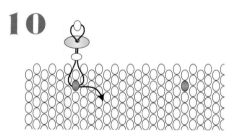

Weave through the edge of the bracelet, bringing the needle out through the second blue bead. Repeat the button process *(Illustration 11)*.

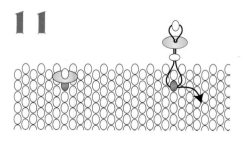

Weave the end of the thread through several rows of stitching to secure. Clip thread close.

Encircle your wrist with a row of goddesses, then fasten the bracelet with simple bead and loop closures!

Reverse and repeat pattern for 2nd half of bracelet

Row 99

Row 1

Beading Pattern

Rows 1 and 2 **beads** 2B 24M 2B
Row 3 (r to l): 1B 12M 1B
Row 4 (l to r): 1B 12M 1B
Row 5 (r to l): 1B 10M 1G 1M 1B
Row 6 (l to r): 1B 11M 1G 1B
Row 7 (r to l): 1B 8M 1G 3M 1B
Row 8 (l to r): 1B 12M 1B
Row 9 (r to l): 1B 5M 1G 6M 1B
Row 10 (l to r): 1B 12M 1B sj
Row 11 (r to l): 1B 2M 1G 9M 1B
Row 12 (l to r): 1B 1M 1G 7M 2G 1M 1B
Row 13 (r to l): 1B 1M 3G 8M 1B
Row 14 (l to r): 1B 8M 2G 1M 1G 1B
Row 15 (r to l): 1B 1G 2M 2G 1M 4G 2M 1B
Row 16 (l to r): 1B 1M 8G 1M 1G 1M 1G
Row 17 (r to l): 1B 1M 11G 1B
Row 18 (l to r): 1B 13G
Row 19 (r to l): 1B 1M 12G
Row 20 (l to r): 1B 13G
Row 21 (r to l): 1B 1M 11G 1B
Row 22 (l to r): 1B 1M 8G 1M 1G 1M 1G
Row 23 (r to l): 1B 1G 2M 2G 1M 4G 2M 1B
Row 24 (l to r): 1B 8M 2G 1M 1G 1B
Row 25 (r to l): 1B 1M 3G 8M 1B
Row 26 (l to r): 1B 1M 1G 7M 2G 1M 1B
Row 27 (r to l): 1B 2M 1G 9M 1B
Row 28 (l to r): 1B 12M 1B
Row 29 (r to l): 1B 12M 1B
Row 30 (l to r): 1B 12M 1B
Row 31 (r to l): 1B 12M 1B
Row 32 (l to r): 1B 12M 1B
Row 33 (r to l): 1B 5M 1G 6M 1B
Row 34 (l to r): 1B 12M 1B
Row 35 (r to l): 1B 12M 1B
Row 36 (l to r): 1B 12M 1B
Row 37 (r to l): 1B 12M 1B
Row 38 (l to r): 1B 11M 1G 1B
Row 39 (r to l): 1B 12M 1B
Row 40 (l to r): 1B 12M 1B
Row 41 (r to l): 1B 12M 1B
Row 42 (l to r): 1B 12M 1B
Row 43 (r to l): 1B 8M 1G 3M 1B
Row 44 (l to r): 1B 12M 1B
Row 45 (r to l): 1B 12M 1B
Row 46 (l to r): 1B 9M 1G 2M 1B
Row 47 (r to l): 1B 12M 1B
Row 48 (l to r): 1B 6M 1G 5M 1B
Row 49 (r to l): 1B 12M 1B

Row 50 (l to r): 1B 12M 1B
Row 51 (r to l): 1B 2M 1G 6M 1G 2M 1B
Row 52 (l to r): 1B 9M 2G 1M 1B
Row 53 (r to l): 1B 1M 3G 8M 1B
Row 54 (l to r): 1B 8M 2G 1M 1G 1B
Row 55 (r to l): 1B 1G 2M 2G 1M 4G 2M 1B
Row 56 (l to r): 1B 1M 8G 1M 1G 1M 1G
Row 57 (r to l): 1B 1M 11G 1B
Row 58 (l to r): 1B 13G
Row 59 (r to l): 1B 1M 12G
Row 60 (l to r): 1B 13G
Row 61 (r to l): 1B 1M 11G 1B
Row 62 (l to r): 1B 1M 8G 1M 1G 1M 1G
Row 63 (r to l): 1B 1G 2M 2G 1M 4G 2M 1B
Row 64 (l to r): 1B 8M 2G 1M 1G 1B
Row 65 (r to l): 1B 1M 3G 8M 1B
Row 66 (l to r): 1B 9M 2G 1M 1B
Row 67 (r to l): 1B 2M 1G 9M 1B
Row 68 (l to r): 1B 12M 1B
Row 69 (r to l): 1B 9M 1G 2M 1B
Row 70 (l to r): 1B 12M 1B
Row 71 (r to l): 1B 12M 1B
Row 72 (l to r): 1B 11M 1G 1B
Row 73 (r to l): 1B 11M 1G 1B
Row 74 (l to r): 1B 12M 1B
Row 75 (r to l): 1B 12M 1B
Row 76 (l to r): 1B 12M 1B
Row 77 (r to l): 1B 12M 1B
Row 78 (l to r): 1B 5M 1G 6M 1B
Row 79 (r to l): 1B 3M 1G 8M 1B
Row 80 (l to r): 1B 12M 1B
Row 81 (r to l): 1B 12M 1B
Row 82 (l to r): 1B 12M 1B
Row 83 (r to l): 1B 8M 1G 3M 1B
Row 84 (l to r): 1B 12M 1B
Row 85 (r to l): 1B 1M 1G 10M 1B
Row 86 (l to r): 1B 12M 1B
Row 87 (r to l): 1B 12M 1B
Row 88 (l to r): 1B 12M 1B
Row 89 (r to l): 1B 10M 1G 1M 1B
Row 90 (l to r): 1B 7M 1G 4M 1B
Row 91 (r to l): 1B 2M 1G 9M 1B
Row 92 (l to r): 1B 9M 2G 1M 1B
Row 93 (r to l): 1B 1M 3G 8M 1B
Row 94 (l to r): 1B 8M 1G 2M 1G 1B
Row 95 (r to l): 1B 1G 2M 2G 1M 4G 2M 1B
Row 96 (l to r): 1B 1M 8G 1M 1G 1M 1G
Row 97 (r to l): 1B 1M 11G 1B
Row 98 (l to r): 1B 13G
Row 99 (r to l): 1B 1M 12G
Rows 100 to 198: Begin at row 98 and work backward

Diva Necklace

Suede

Samples made by Elizabeth Harkins and Sandy Pardo

Finished size: approximately 1" x 6" with fringe

General Materials

19 mm wood bead • 6" piece of garment weight suede • Assorted beads for fringe, arms and strap • 36" of .010 49-strand flexible beading wire • Beading thread and needle • Polyester fiberfill

Gold Diva
Toho Beads:
3 grams 11/0 #1 • 3 grams 11/0 #2 • 7 grams 11/0 #2C (head) • 3 grams 11/0 #423

Purple Diva
Toho Beads:
4 grams 11/0 #252 (head) • 5 grams 11/0 #136C (hair) • 1 gram 11/0 #935 (top of skirt) • 6 grams 11/0 #461 (fringe)

Black Diva
Toho Beads:
10 grams 11/0 #610 (head) • 5 grams 11/0 #29AF (hair) • 5 grams 11/0 #9B (top of skirt) • 5 grams 11/0 #558 (fringe)

The instructions given are for the basic doll, hair and fringe. Let the samples inspire you to try different types of patterns and fringe on your own necklace.

Let's Begin

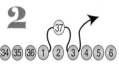

1 Pour a few size 11/0 beads into a small shallow bowl or beading tray. Cut a 48" length of thread, thread the needle with one end. String 36 beads on the thread and slide them down to within 6" of the other end. Pass the needle back through all of the beads again to form a circle *(Illustration 1)*. Bring the needle out just after the first bead strung. (This way the tail won't interfere with the first few stitches!)

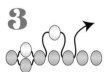

2 **Row 2:**
Thread on a bead, skip the next bead in the row and thread the needle through the second bead *(Illustration 2)*.

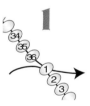

3 Thread on another bead, skip the next bead in the row and thread the needle through the second bead *(Illustration 3)*.

Notice how the beads from the original circle 'share' the space with the new beads? Try to adjust your tension so that the row looks more or less like Illustration 4. To keep the beads from twisting, hold the circle of beads between your thumb and forefinger. Continue adding beads in this fashion to the end of the row. (18 beads total)

4

Row 3: Do you see where your thread has come out of the last bead of Row 2?

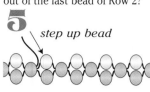

5 *step up bead*

It's smack dab against the first bead of Row 2 *(Illustration 5)*. This first bead is called the 'step up' bead. You have to 'step up' through it to begin the next row *(Illustration 6)*.

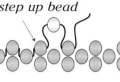

6 *step up bead*

You'll begin every row this way. As you can see, the beads from Row 2 are higher than the rest. In Row 3 we'll place a bead in between each of these higher ones. Thread on a bead and pass your needle through the next high bead as shown in Illustration 7. Continue adding beads in this manner to the end of the row. There should be 18 beads total in the row.

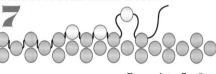

7

8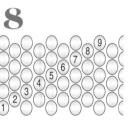

Rows 4 to 5: Step up at the beginning of each row, then add a bead between each of the beads from the previous row. You will be adding 18 beads on every row. Keep your tension consistent.

Here's a hint to help you count the rows - count on the diagonal as shown in Illustration 8.

Let's face facts:

You're going to run out of thread at some point, but there's no need to panic - or to tie a knot! To end a thread, weave up and down through a few beads on the rows below. Clip thread end. Cut a 36" length of thread and weave up and down through a few beads to come out of the last bead you added. Weave down to end a thread, weave up to start a new one *(Illustration 9)*.

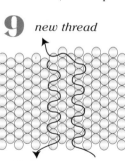

9 *new thread*

old thread

Let's check the fit.

Slip the beaded ring over the fattest part of the wood bead. It should fit snugly. If the bead ring is too small, check to see if the tension on your first few rows is a bit tight. If that's the case, simply add a couple of rows to the working end and remove the first few rows of stitching. If your ring slips easily over the bead, that's OK. It will stay in place after a few rows of decreasing.

Now, lets work the top and bottom of the bead.

A note about the illustrations.
The illustrations are drawn as if you were looking down from the top of the bead.

Row 6: Add 5 beads as usual, then make the next stitch without a bead (decrease). Repeat two more times. Step up to begin the next row *(Illustration 10)*.

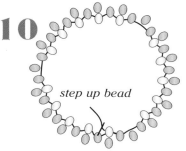

step up bead

Row 7: Add a bead between each of the beads of the previous row. Step up to begin the next row *(Illustration 11)*.

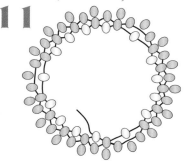

Row 8: Add a bead between each of the beads of the previous row. Step up to begin the next row *(Illustration 12)*.

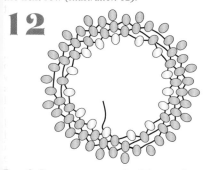

Row 9: Decrease over each of the previous decreases as shown in Illustration 13. Beading sequence:
Add three beads, decrease, add four beads, decrease, add four beads, decrease, add one bead, step up to begin next row.

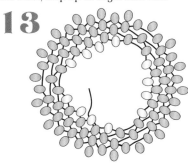

Samples made by Elizabeth Harkins and Sandy Pardo

Row 10: Add a bead between each of the beads of the previous row. Step up to begin the next row *(Illustration 14)*.

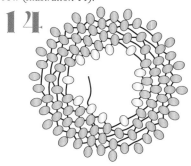

Row 11: Add a bead between each of the beads of the previous row. Step up to begin next row *(Illustration 15)*.

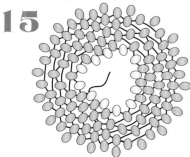

Row 12: Add a bead between every other bead of the previous row *(Illustration 16)*. Weave thread back through this row once more and then through several rows of stitching to secure.

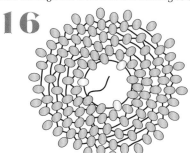

Work the other side of the bead.
Weave thread back through all beadwork until it emerges from the bottom of the original 5-row peyote ring. Repeat Rows 6 to 12 to complete the other half. *It may be helpful to work a few rows on one side of the bead and then work a few on the other side to secure the beading to the form.*

Body Pattern

Shoulder Fold

Doll Body
Cut 1
On Fold

Body: Transfer the body pattern to the wrong side of a piece of garment weight suede. Cut out, fold right sides together where indicated and stitch (by hand or machine) side seams with a ¼" seam allowance. Turn right side out and stuff body lightly with fiberfill or cotton. Whipstitch the bottom closed.

Continued on page 32.

These party girls are equally at home swinging through the jungle or hanging out at an elegant soiree!

Diva Necklace

Continued from page 25.

Beading the Skirt

Skirt: Lightly mark a line around the body ½" up from the bottom. Cut a 36" long piece of beading thread. Thread the beading needle with one end. Pick up four 11/0 seed beads and stitch them to the bottom of the body piece along the marked line as shown in Illustration 17.

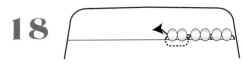

Pick up two more seed beads and continue stitching along the marked line as shown in Illustration 18. Continue to add groups of two beads completely around the bottom of the body. Keep a very light tension throughout.

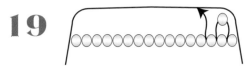

When you have completed stitching the circle, pass your needle back through the first bead. Now, we are going to peyote stitch the rest of the skirt. Pick up a bead, skip the second bead in the circle and pass your needle through the third bead *(Illustration 19)*.

19

Continue to peyote stitch as you did for the head bead until your stitching is just above the bottom of the body piece. Do not make any decreases as you stitch *(Illustration 20)*.

20

Fringe: Now instead of adding a bead between each of the beads of the previous row, we'll be adding a strand of fringe. Thread on the number of beads you wish for the strand, then add a seed bead. Skip the last seed bead and pass your needle back through all the beads in the strand. Pass your needle through the next high bead of the previous row of stitching *(Illustration 21)*.
Repeat for each strand.

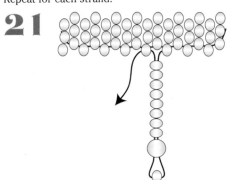

Skirt Front: Use Illustration 22 as a general guide for shaping the skirt front. Your actual bead counts will vary.

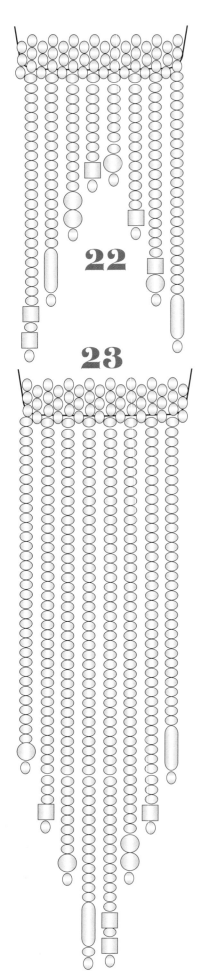

Skirt Back: Use Illustration 23 as a general guide for shaping the skirt back. Your actual bead counts will vary.

Inside Fringe: Flip the skirt over and stitch this row of fringe to the bottom of the body as shown in Illustration 24.

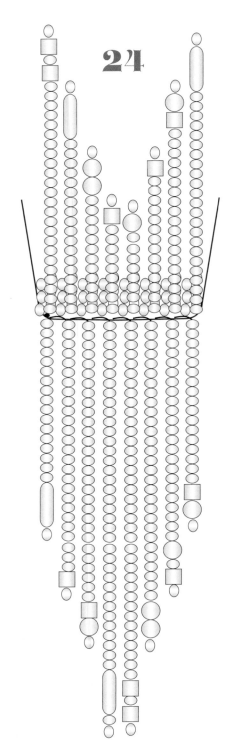

Hair: Most of the doll's hair is fringe that is stitched between the beads of the top row of the head. You might want to make the fringe at the front of the head shorter than at the back, but make your doll's hair any length and style you wish. *(Illustration 25)*
For even fuller hair add fringe between the beads of the next-to-last row of stitching.

25

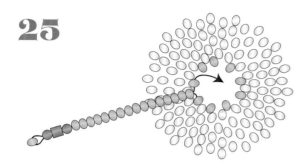

Attaching the Head: Thread on beads for a long strand of hair. Pass your needle down the length of the head bead and make a stitch at the neck. Pass the needle back up the head, tightening the stitch *(Illustration 26)*. Make several of these stitches to secure the head to the body. Force the beads to fill the hole through the head bead. This helps to make the head less wobbly.

26

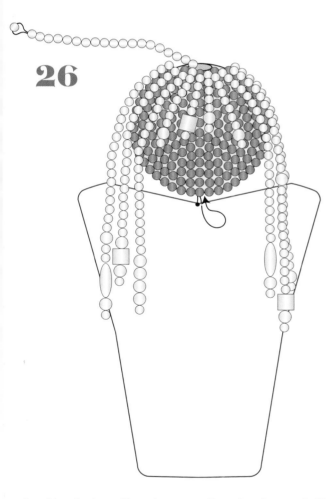

Attaching the Arms: Use a darning needle to thread a strand of beading wire through the suede at a shoulder point. Secure one end of the wire to the shoulder with a knot. Remove the needle and thread the beads for the arm, strap and other arm.
Rethread the wire through the darning needle and pierce the suede at the opposite shoulder. Tie the beading wire to the suede to secure.

Samples made by Elizabeth Harkins and Sandy Pardo

Divine Halo Diva

Samples made by
Eileen Maki

Combine assorted beads and wire to make little divas… simply divine!

Finished size is 2½" x 2½"

General Materials

12mm bead for head • 9mm disk bead for neck • 6" piece of 18 gauge wire • 12" of 26 gauge wire • Pin back • Cotton balls or polyester fiberfill • Round-nose pliers • Beading thread and needle

Green & Black Goddess
Toho Beads:
6 grams 11/0 #560F • 1 gram 11/0 #610 • Six 6/0 #610 • 8 small Brass bicones

Purple Goddess
Toho Beads:
6 grams 11/0 #461 • 1 gram 11/0 #610 • Eight 3.3 treasure beads #705 • Six 6/0 #610

Gold Goddess
Toho Beads:
6 grams 11/0 #103 • 1 gram 11/0 #222 • Six 6/0 #222 • 8 small Brass bicones

Rows 1 & 2: This project is worked in 2 drop peyote stitch - we'll always be working with pairs of beads. Pour a few of the lighter beads into a small shallow bowl or beading tray. Cut a 48" length of thread; thread the needle with one end. Make an overhand knot around a bead about 12" from the end as shown in Illustration 1. Be sure to leave a 12" tail. String 68 beads on the thread.

Row 3: Pick up two more beads and pass the needle back through the second pair of beads from the end *(Illustration 2)*.

2

3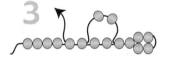

Add two more beads as shown in Illustration 3.

Add two more beads *(Illustration 4)*. Notice how the beads from the first row 'share' the space with the new beads?

4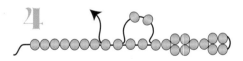

Add a total of 17 groups of 2 beads along the first row. When you reach the end of the row, reverse direction and add the first pair of Row 4 as shown in Illustration 5.

5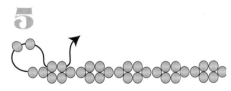

Continue to add pairs of beads to the end of the row as shown in Illustration 6.

6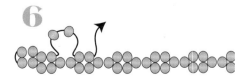

7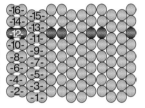

Here's a tip to help you determine which row you are on: count the rows along the edge as shown in Illustration 7.

Work Rows 5 to 11 with light beads.
Work Row 12 with Black beads.
Work Rows 13 to 16 with light beads. The complete beading pattern for the body can be found at the bottom of page 35.

8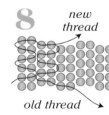

new thread

old thread

You're going to run out of thread at some point, but there's no need to panic - or to tie a knot! To end a thread, weave down through a few beads on the rows below and clip the end. Weave the new thread up through a few beads to come up out of the last bead you added. Weave down to end a thread, weave up to start a new one *(Illustration 8)*.

9

Arms: Turn a loop in one end of the 18 gauge wire using round-nose pliers *(Illustration 9)*.

Thread a 6/0, two Brass bicones or 3.3 treasure beads, a 6/0, two 8/0 and another 6/0 for each side as shown in Illustration 10.

10